SIREN HEAD COLORING BOOK

THIS BOOK BELONGS TO:

- -

- -

Thank you for choosing our Siren Head Coloring Book For Kids
It's great that that you like coloring books as much as we do!

These pages offer hours of fun and are a great way to improve your focus and concentration.

Once you complete the book, there will be a certificate of completion waiting for you as a reward.

Have fun and enjoy!

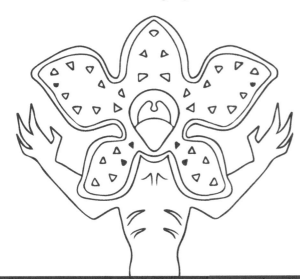

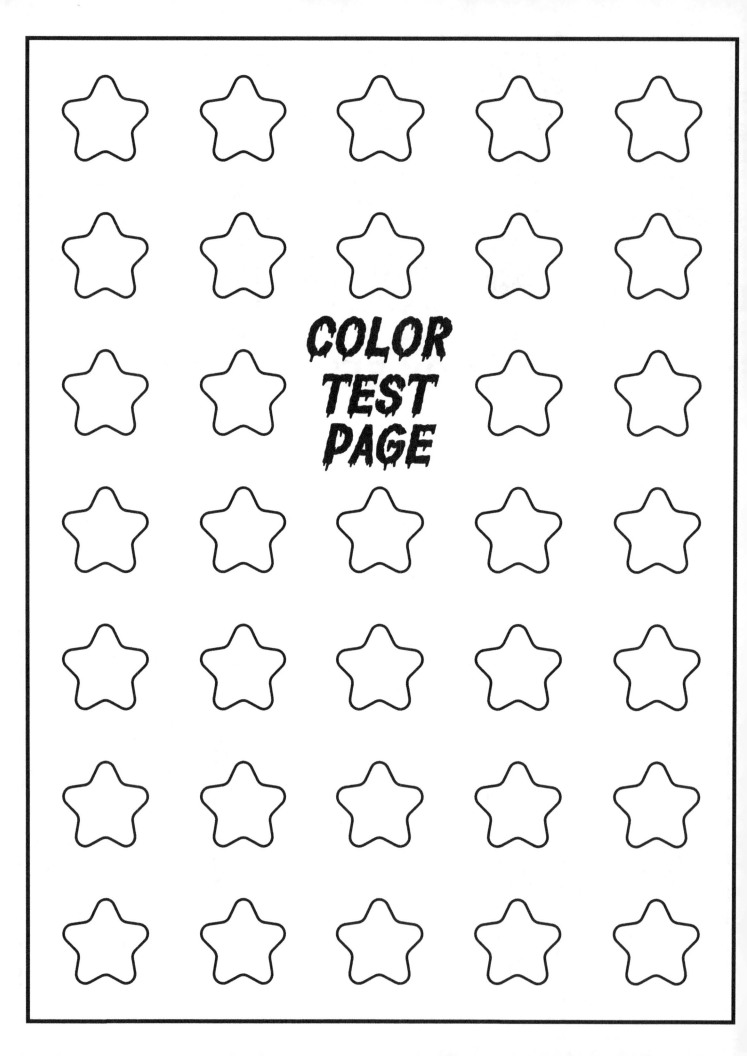

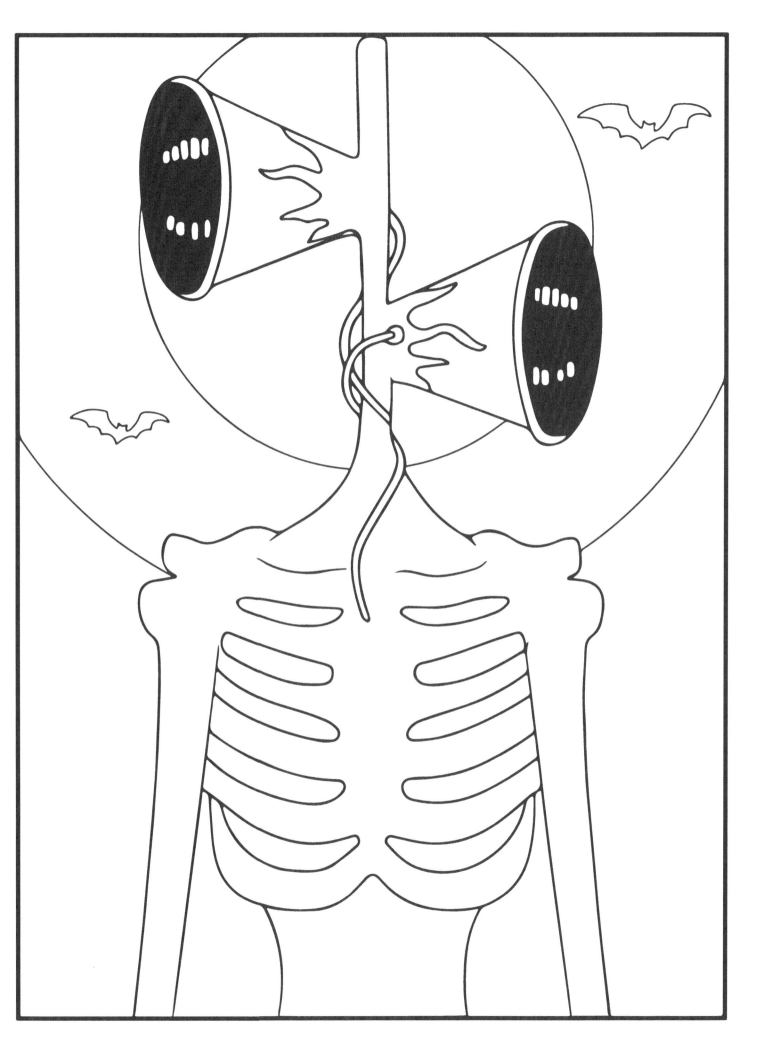

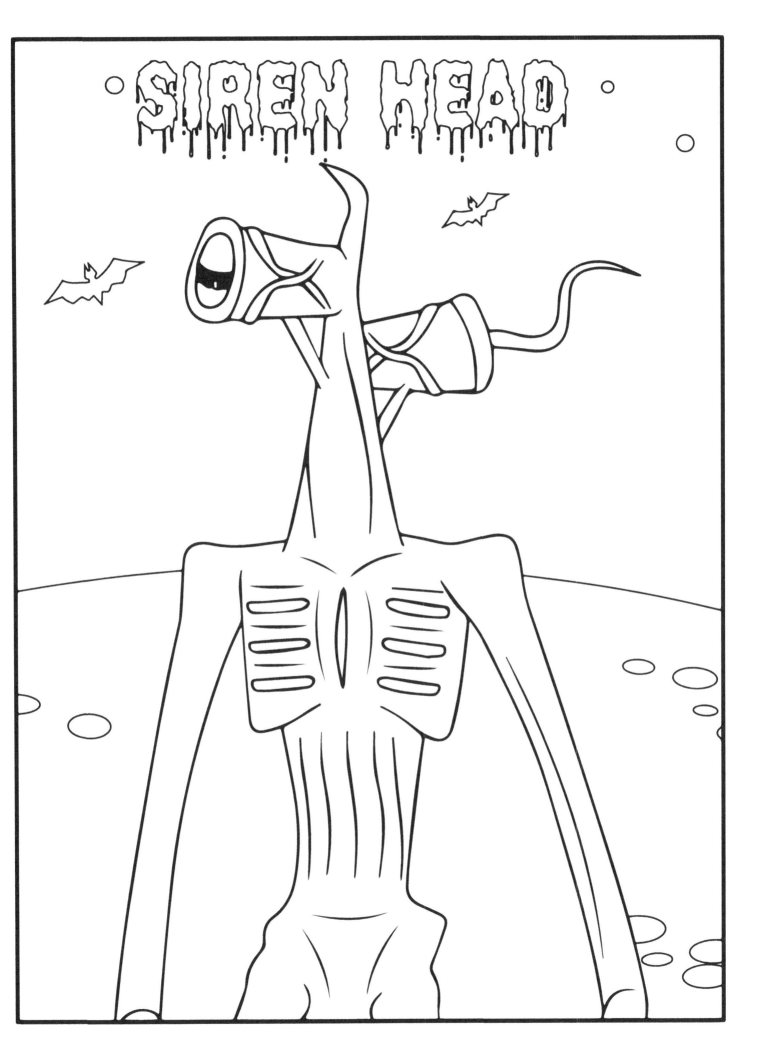

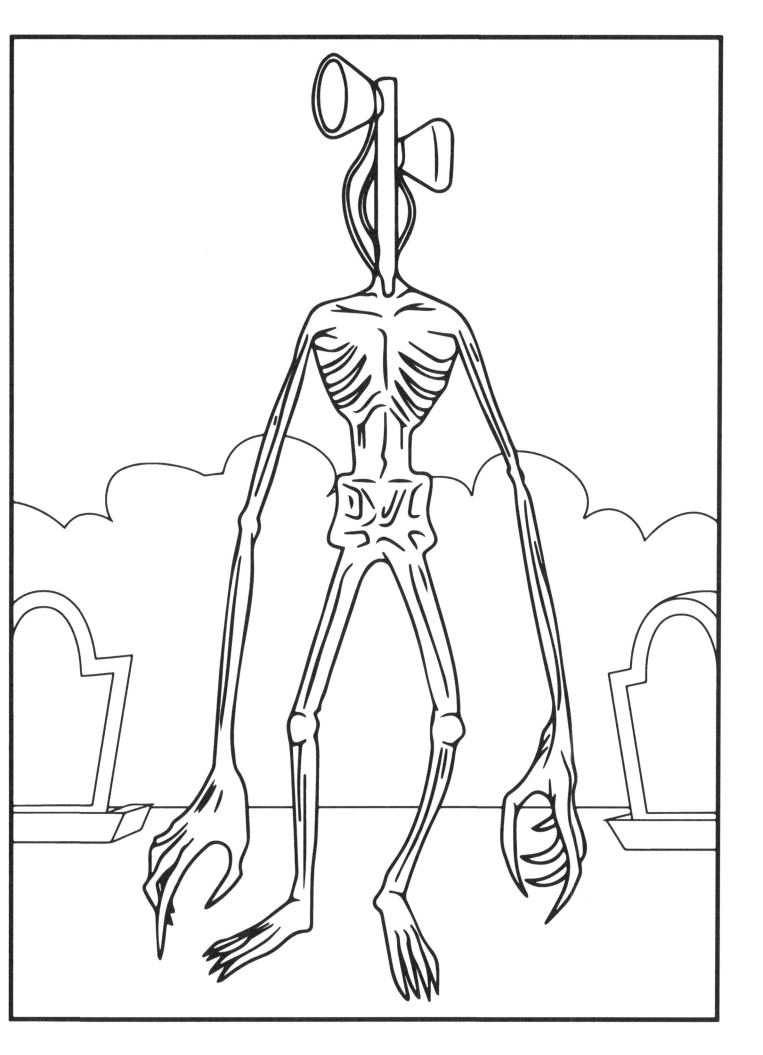

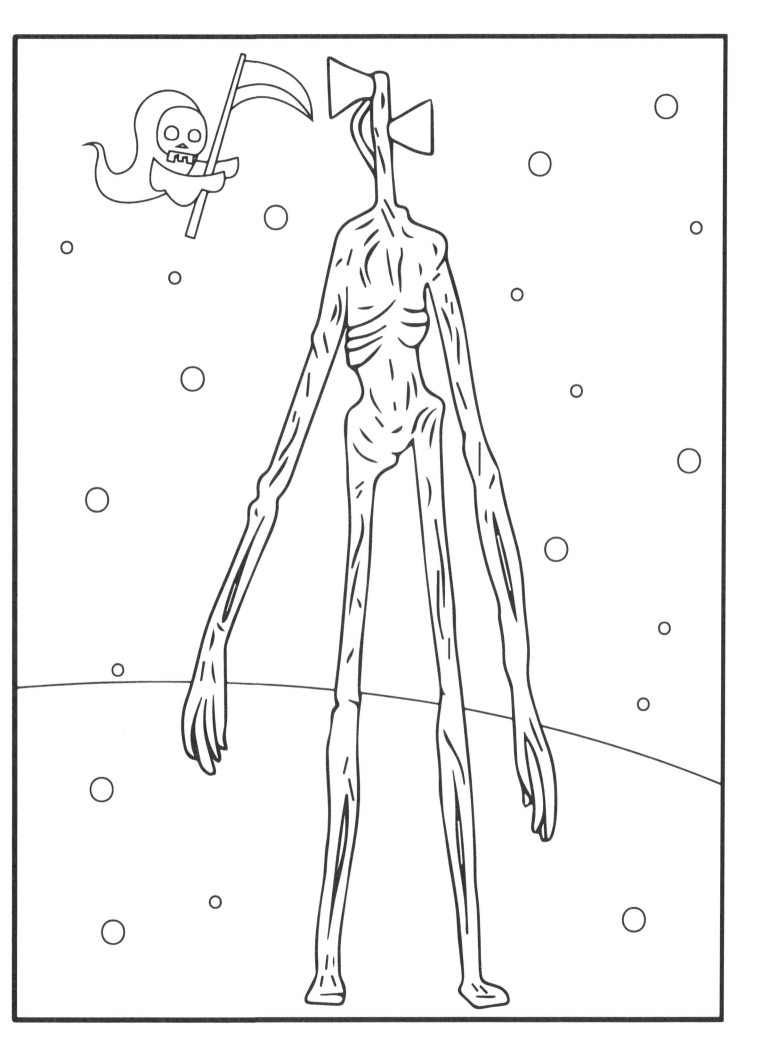

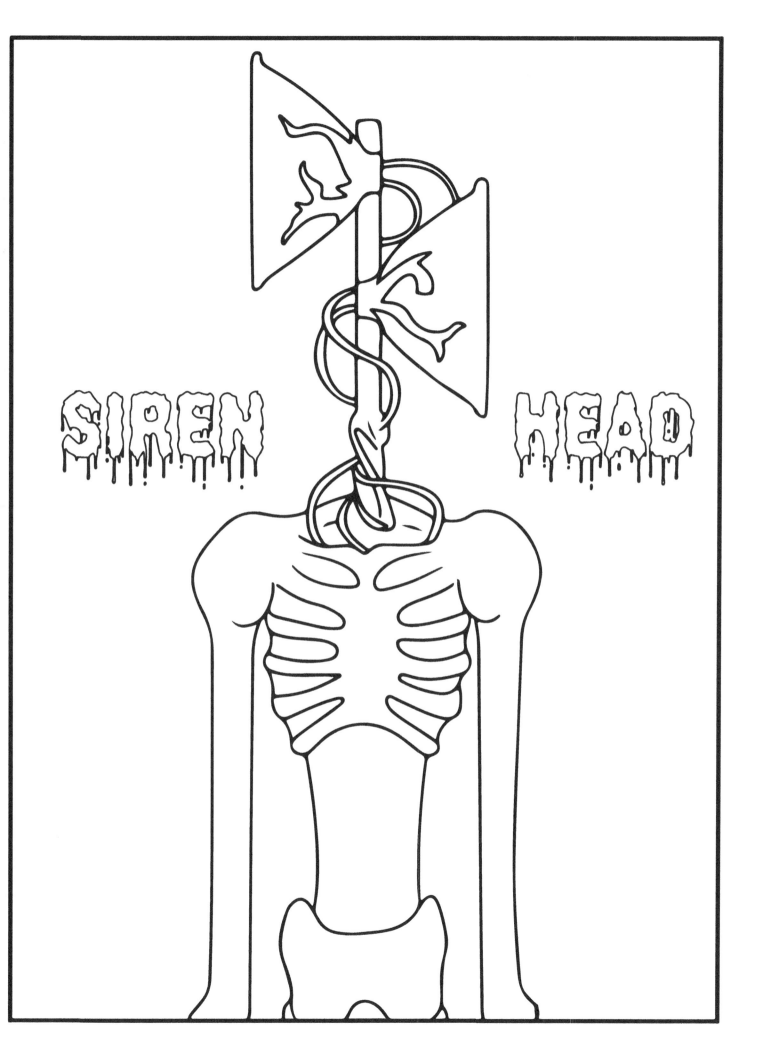

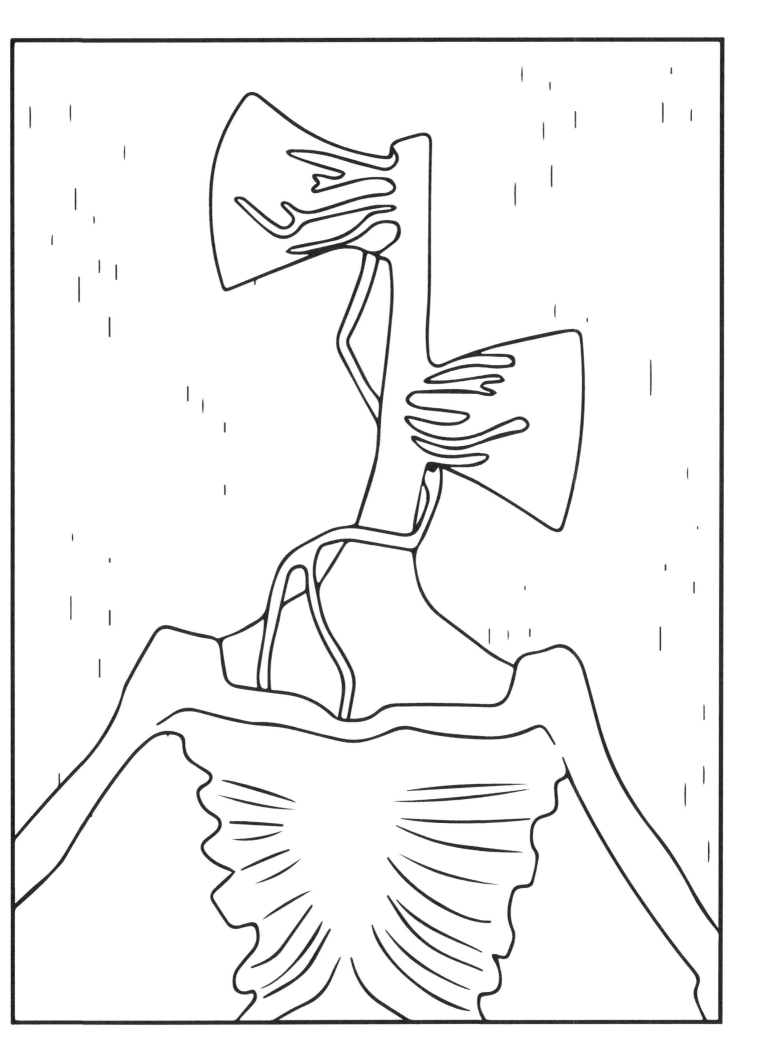

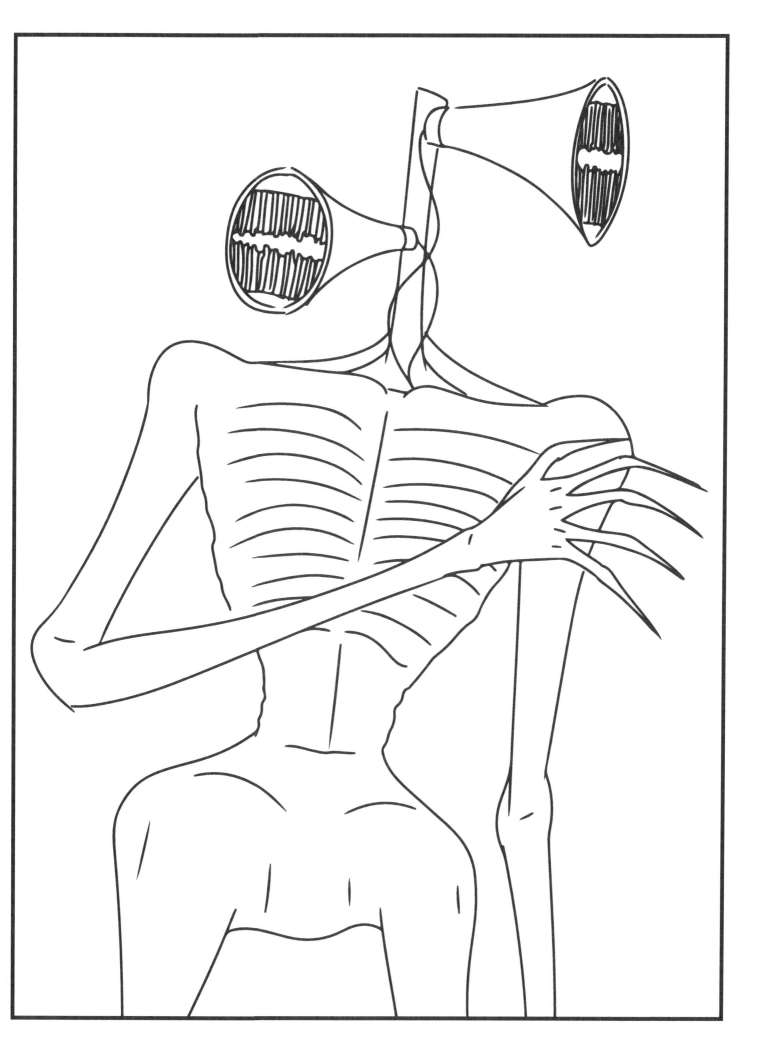

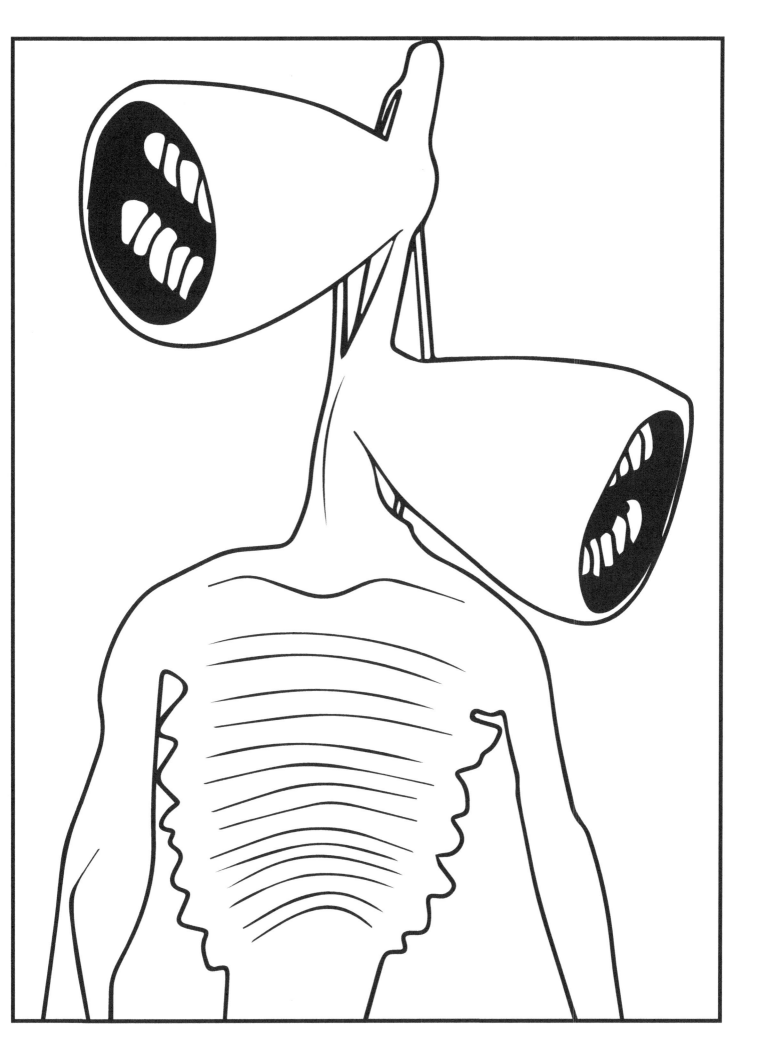

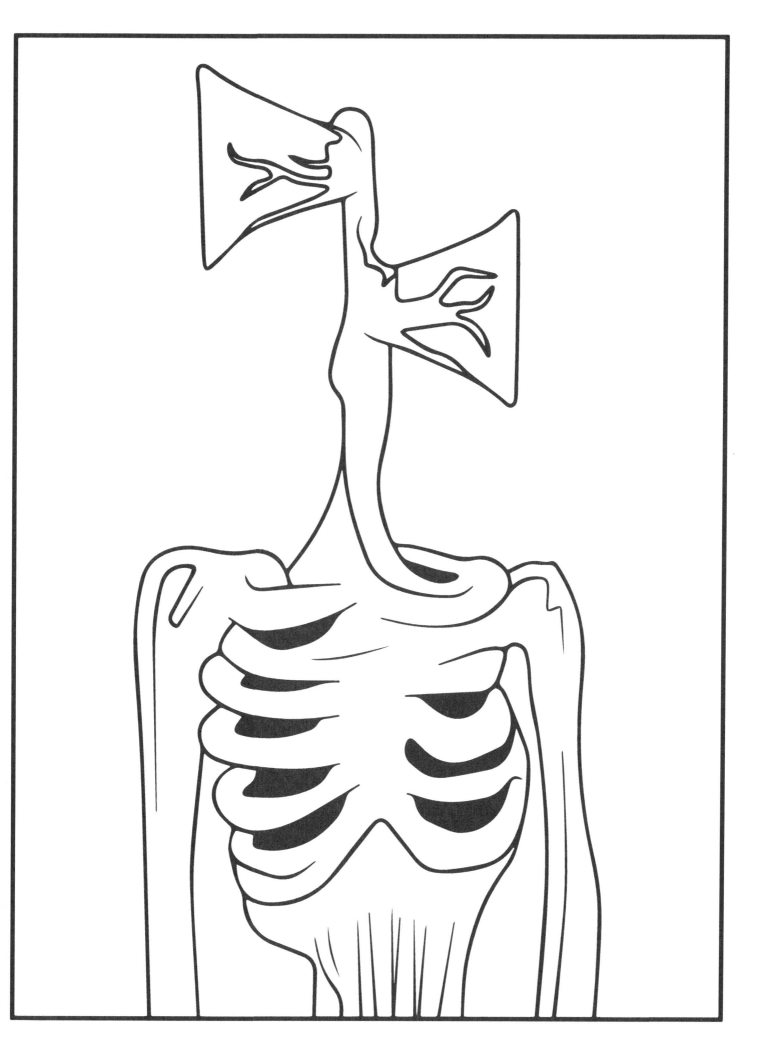

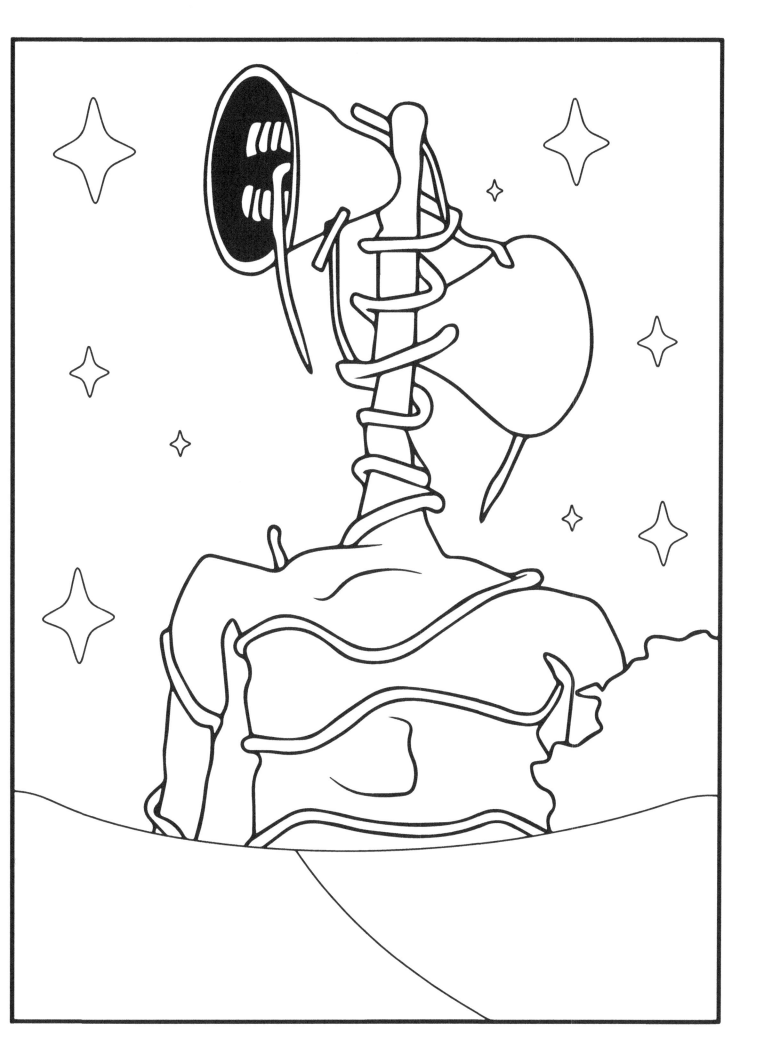

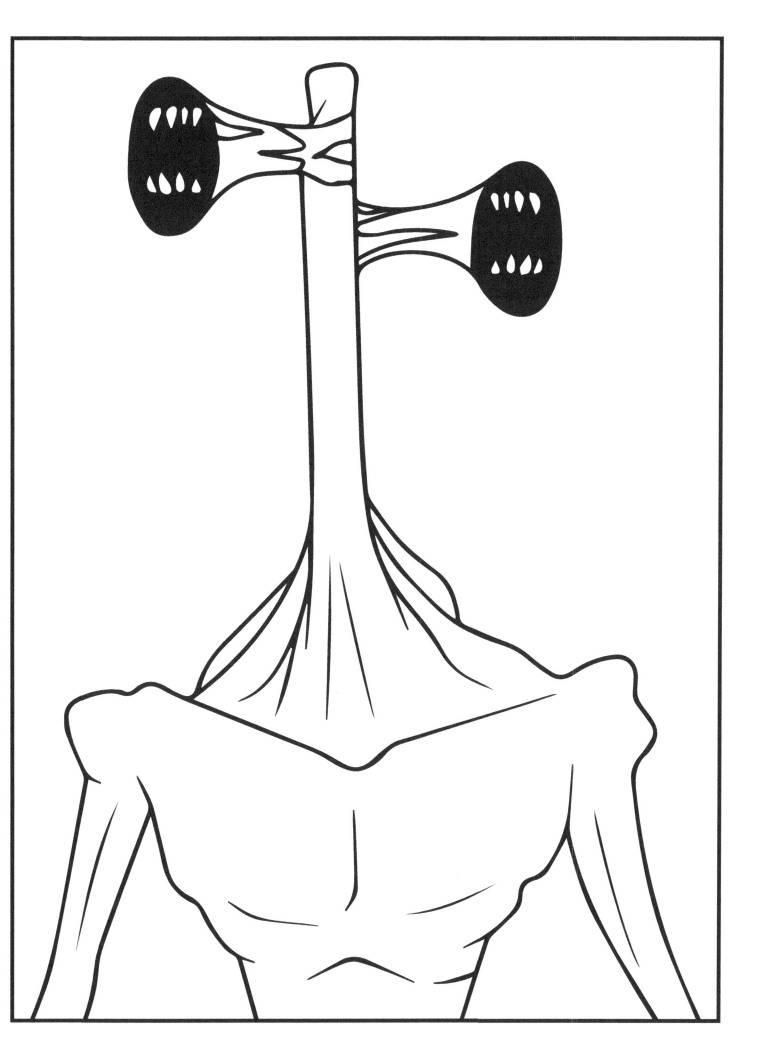

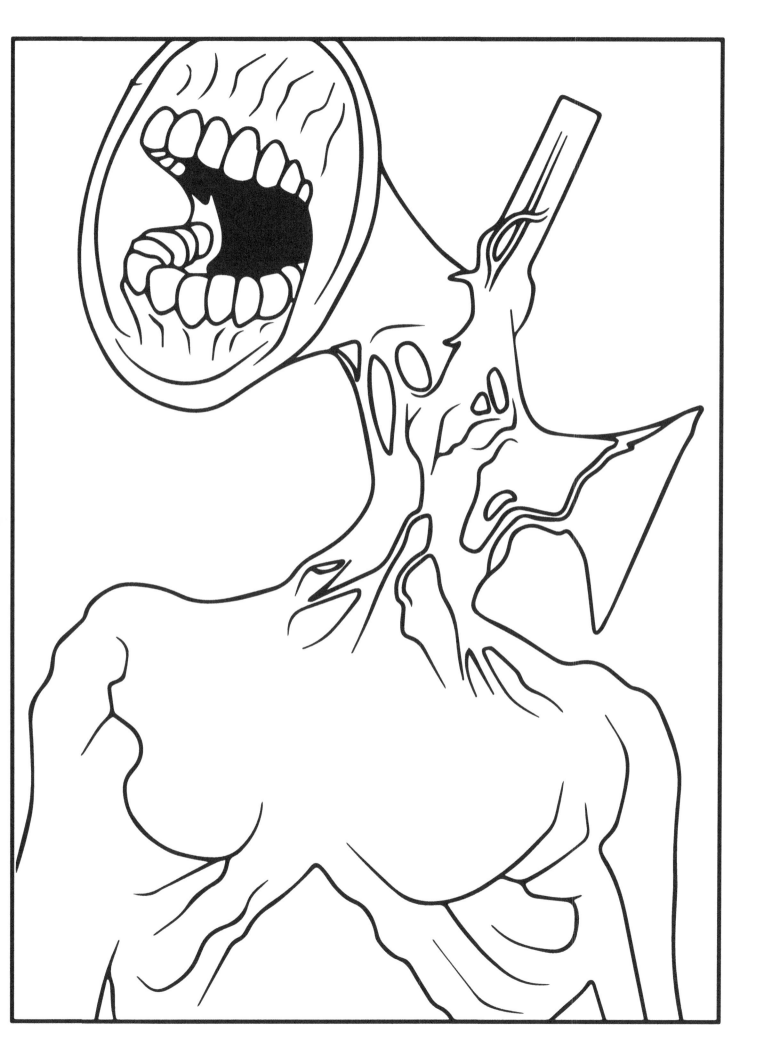

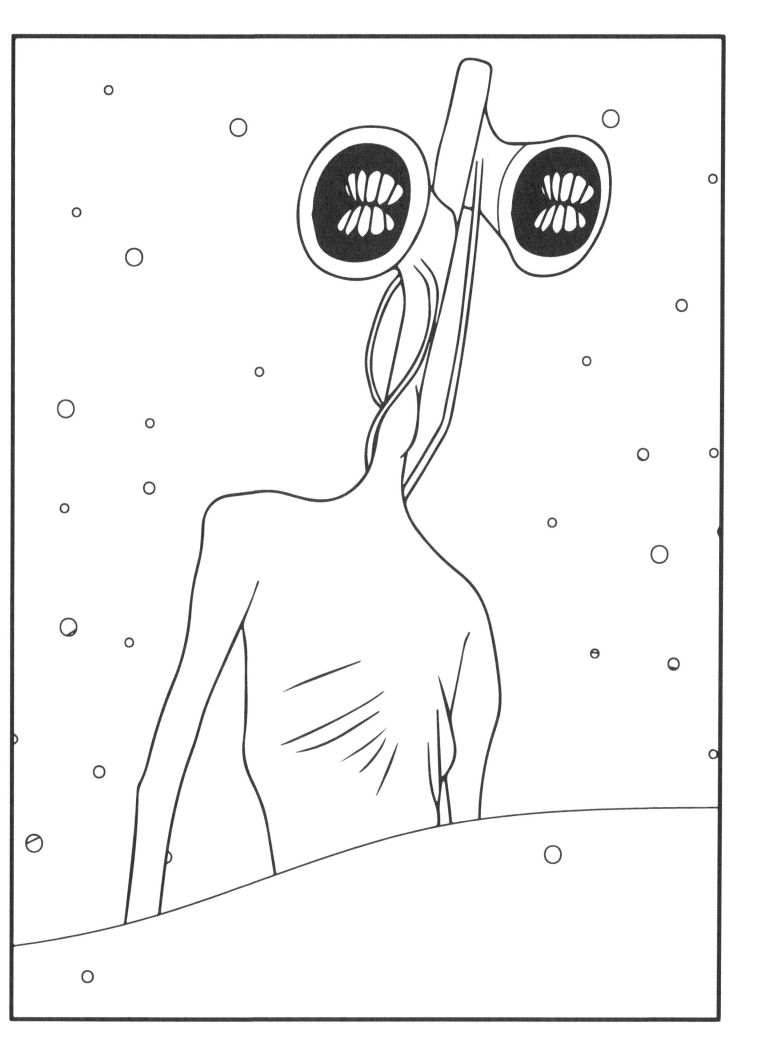

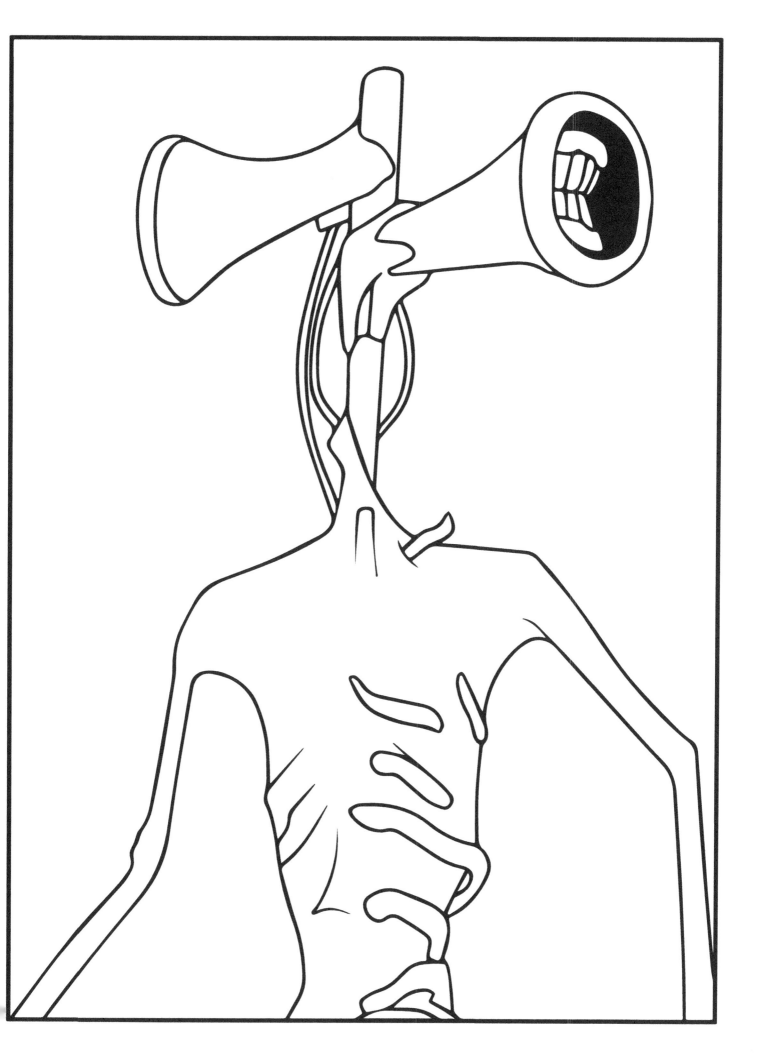

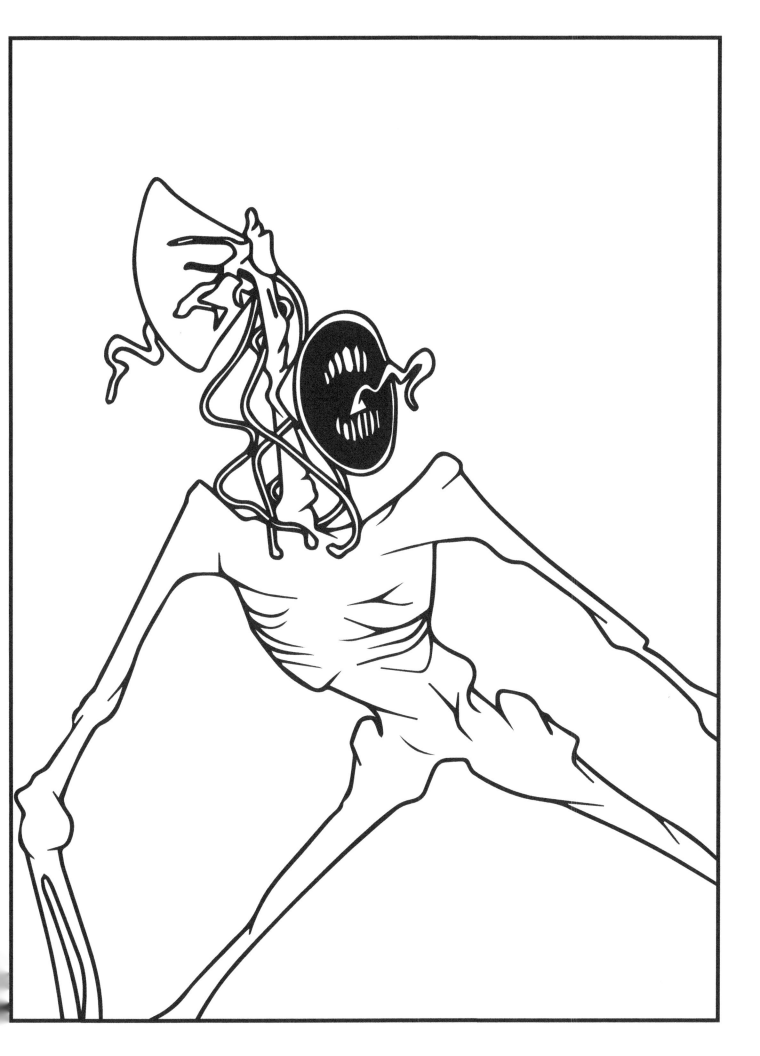

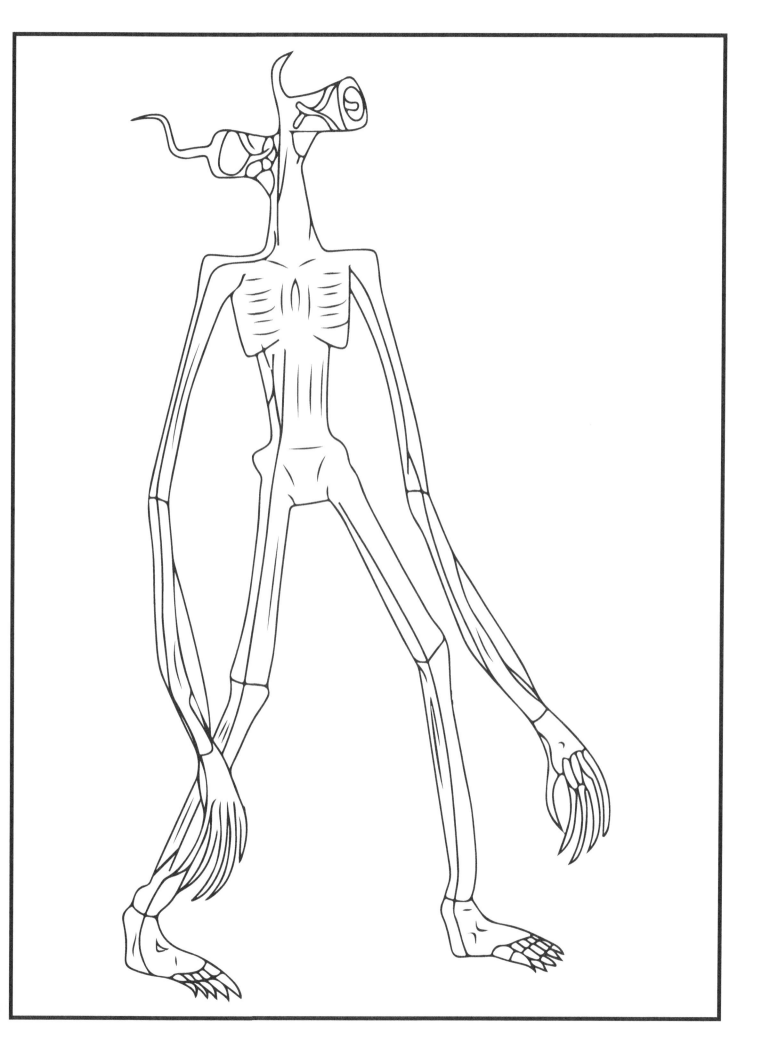

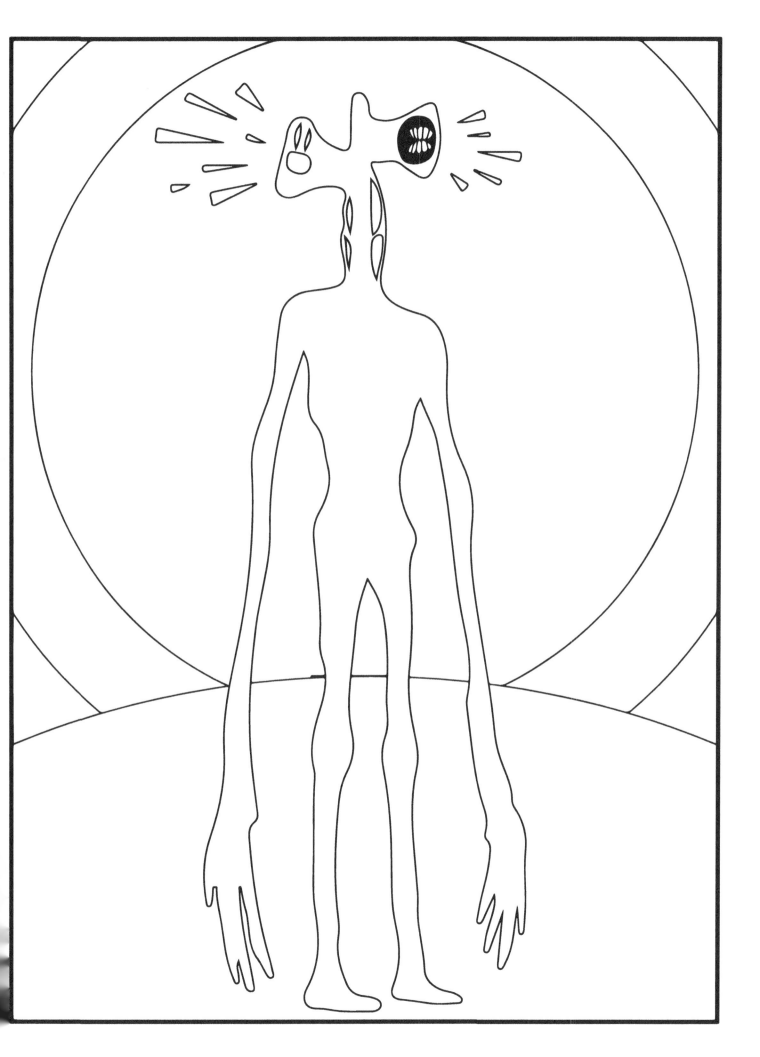

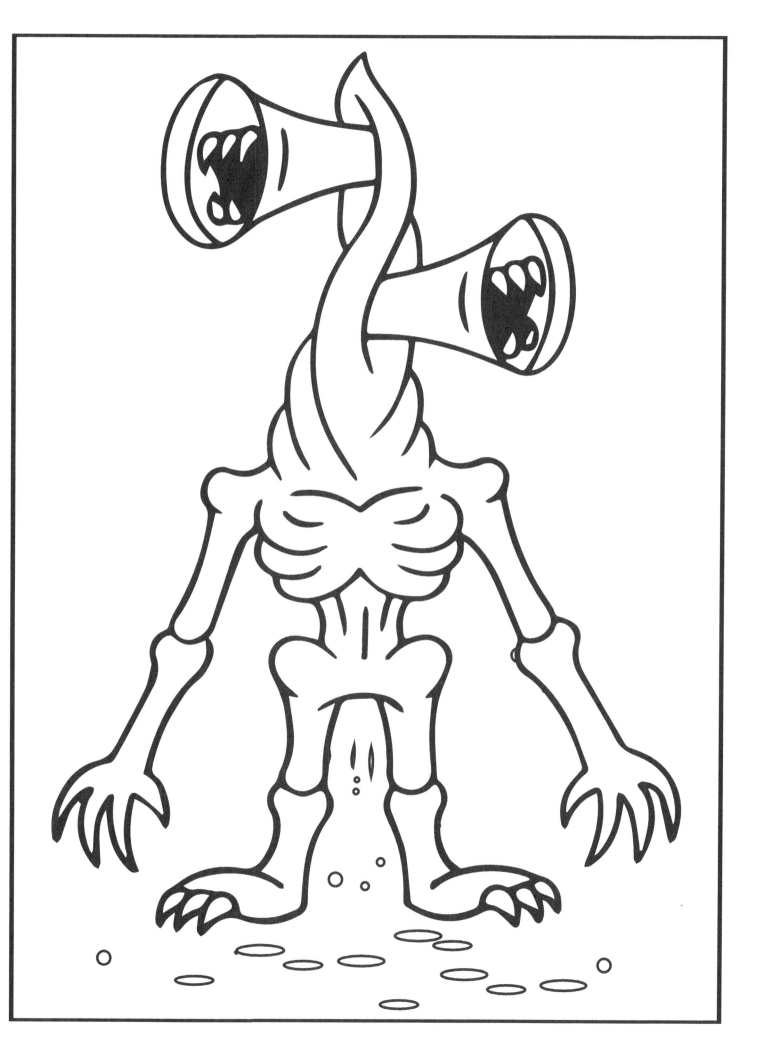

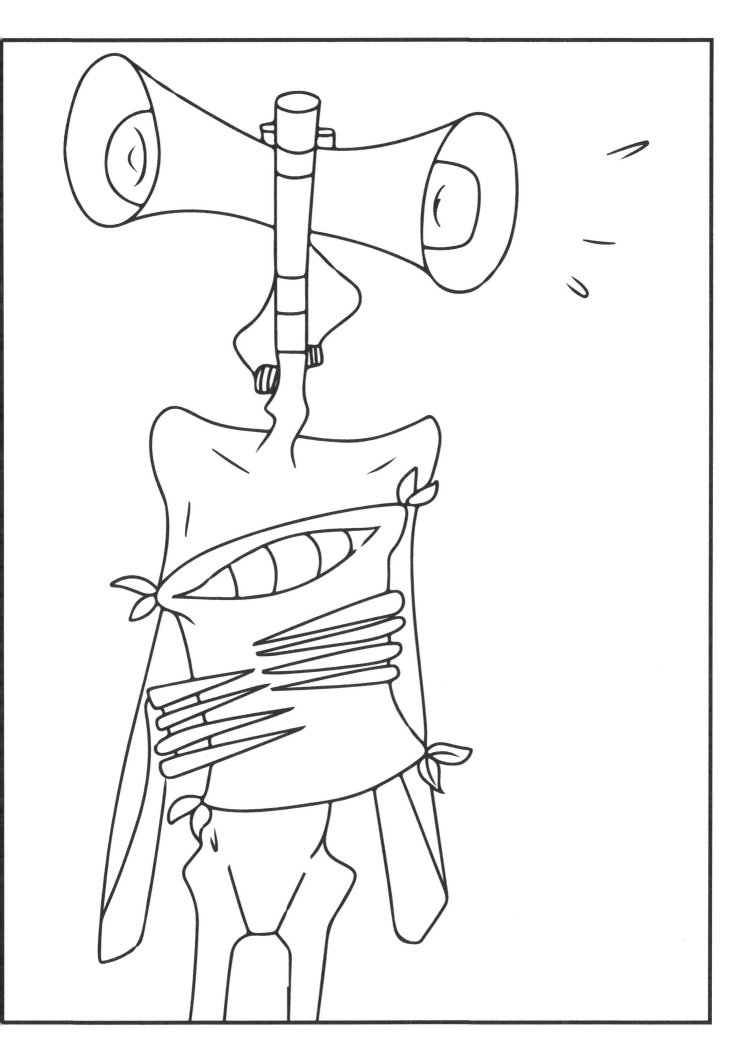

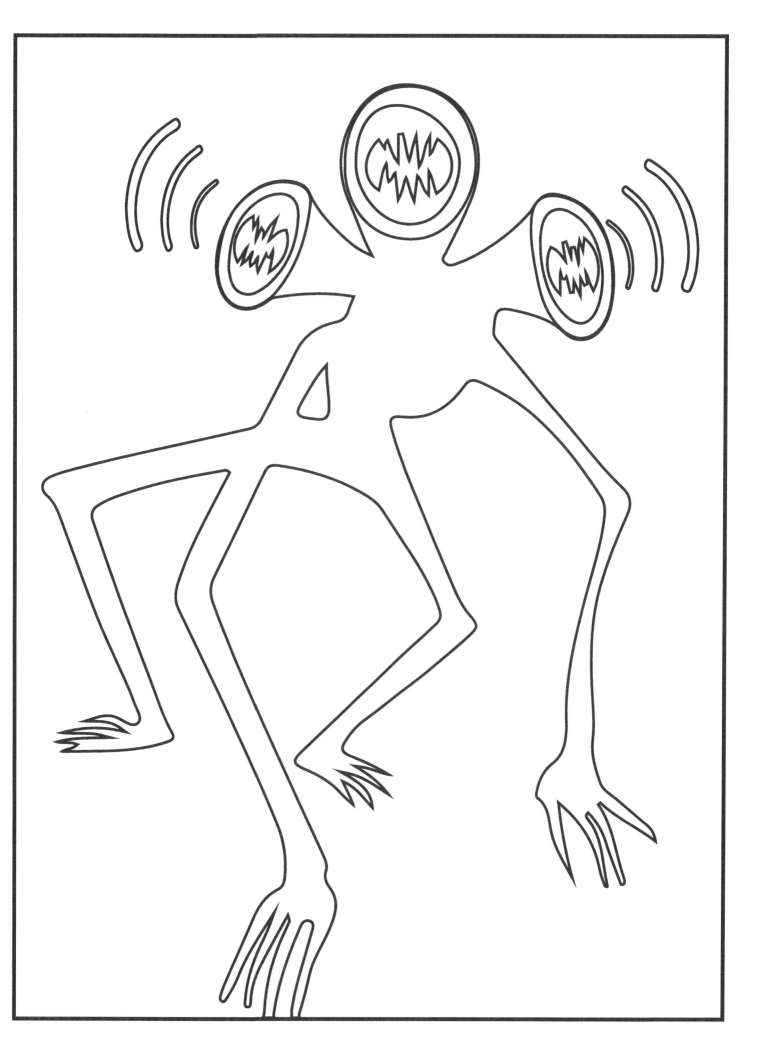

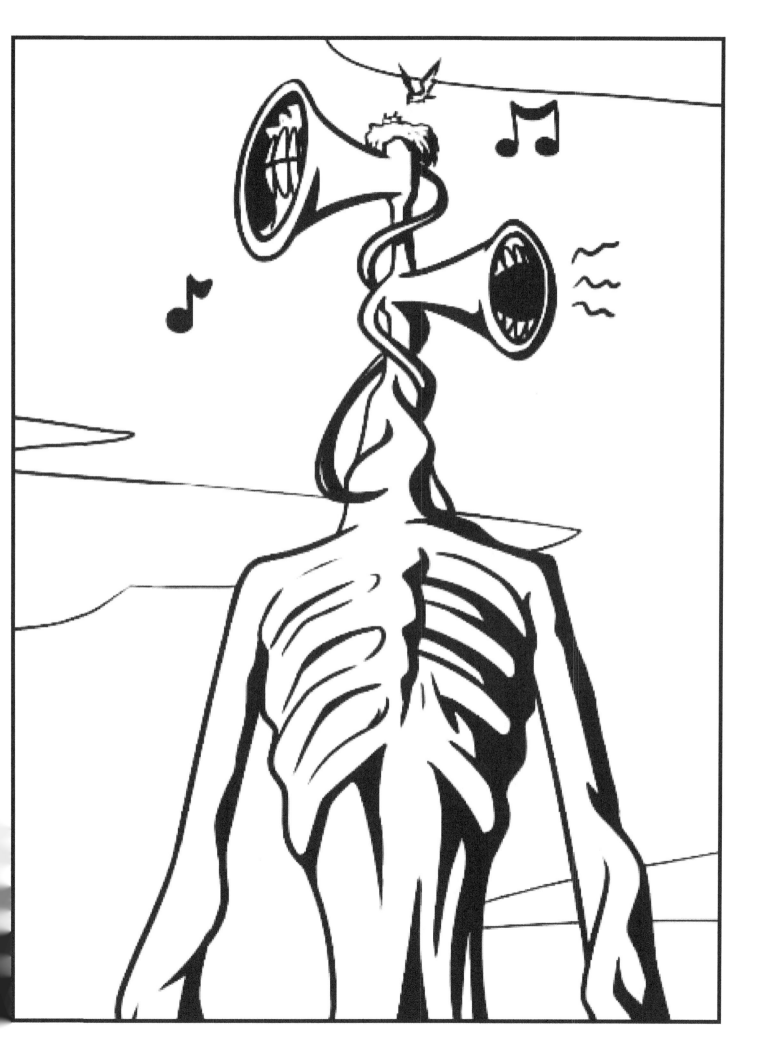

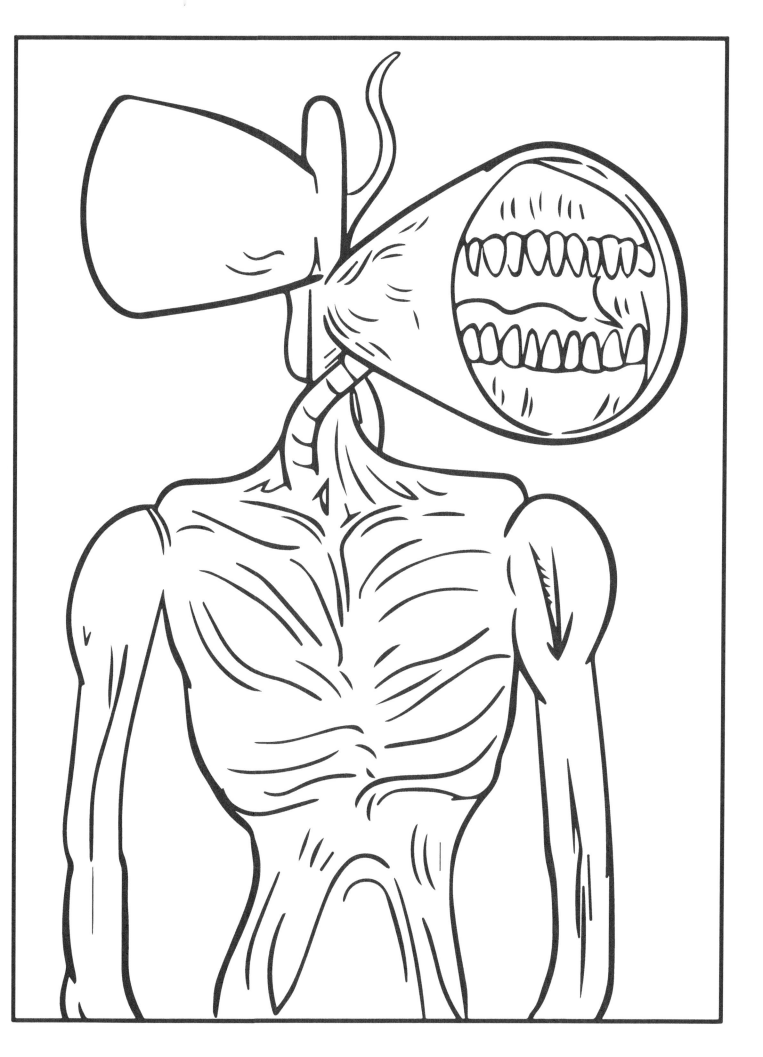

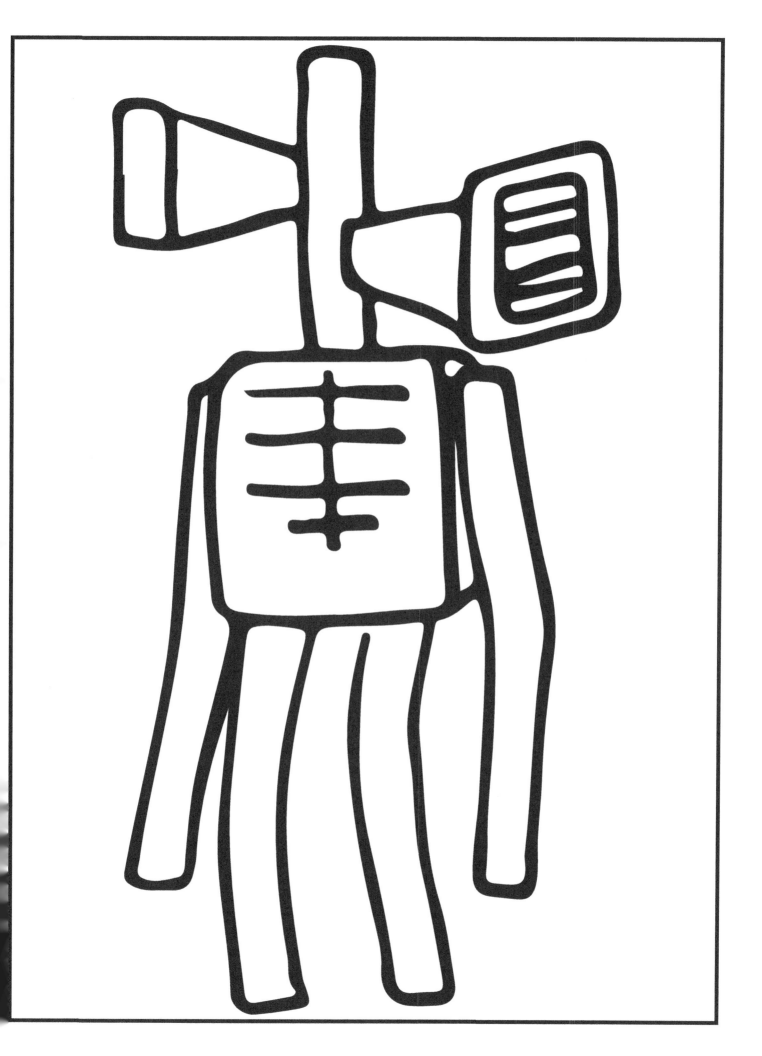

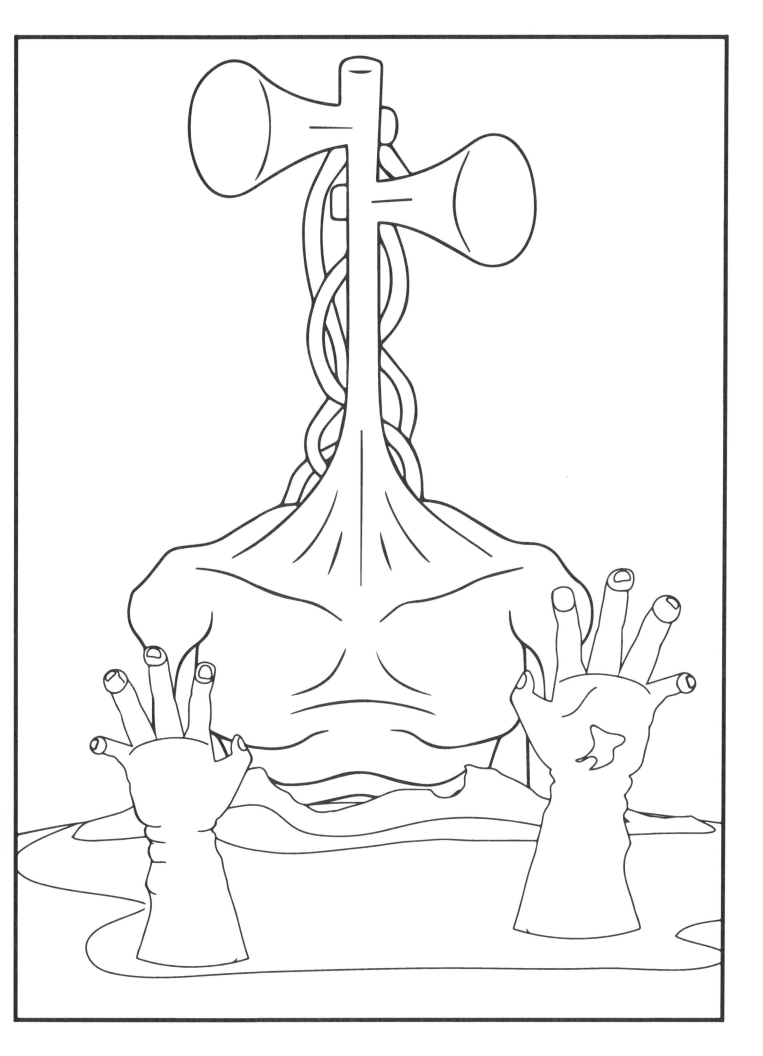

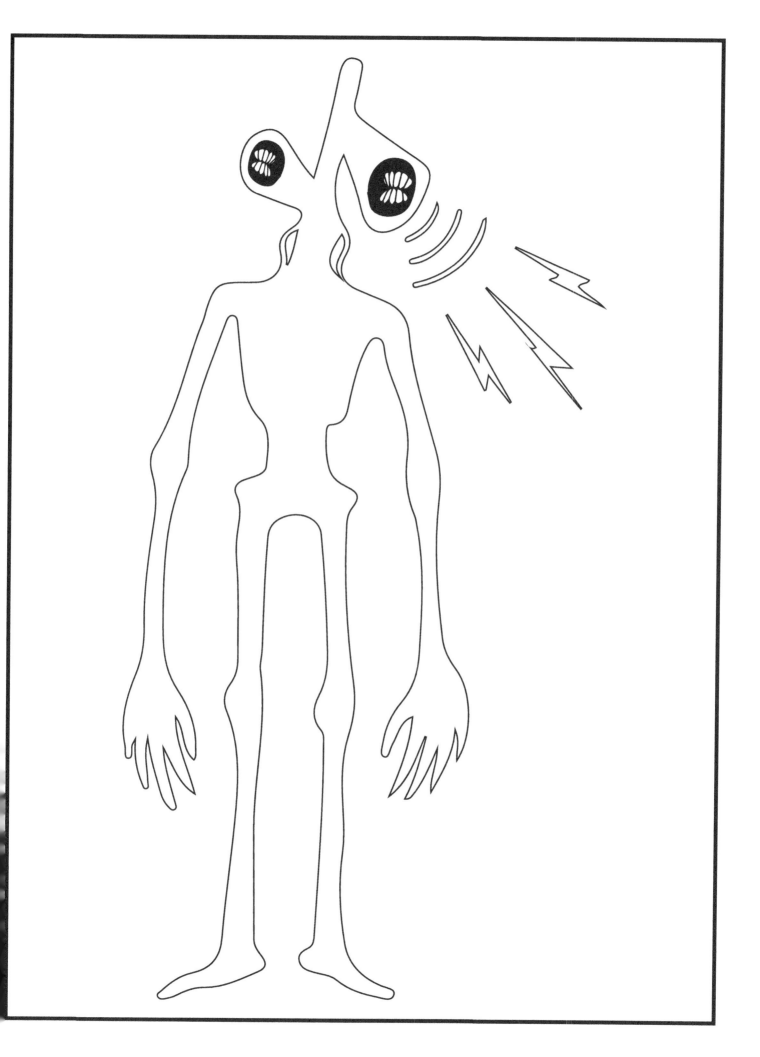

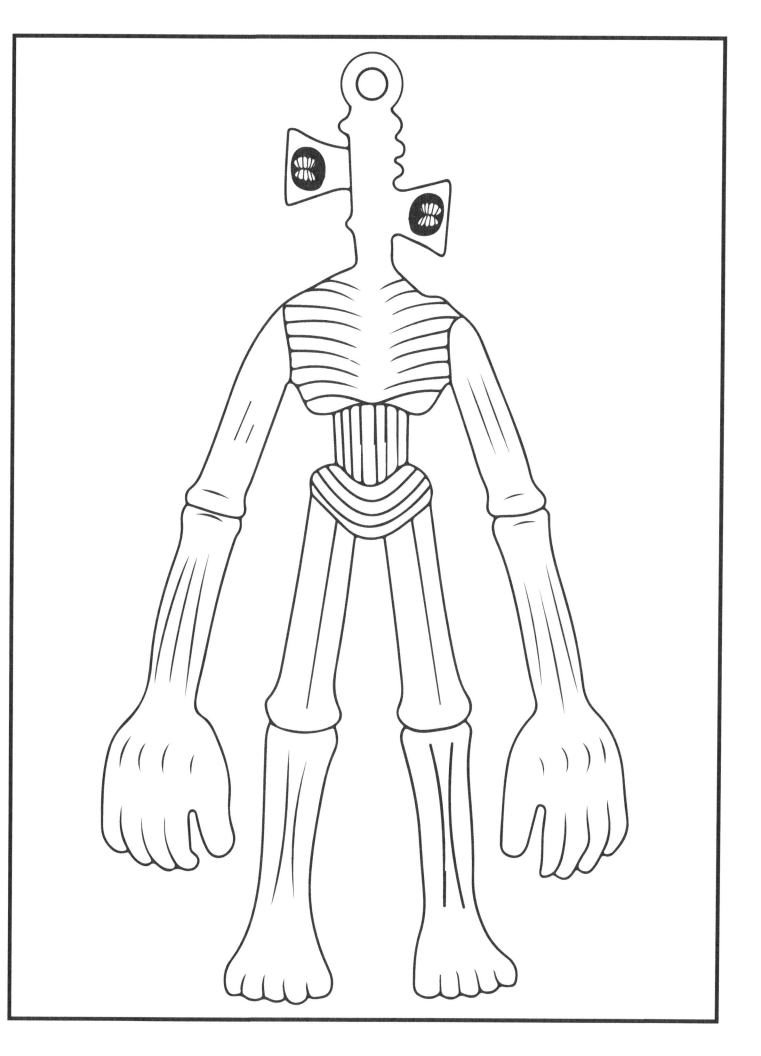

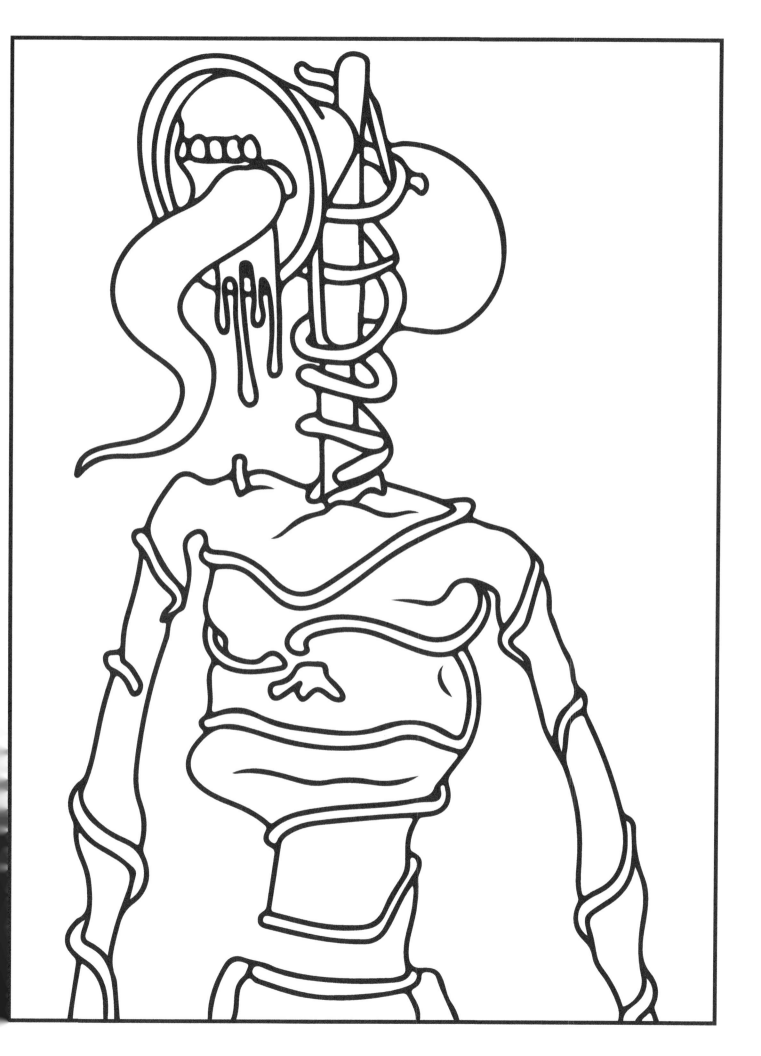

DUAA PRESS PUBLISHING

CERTIFICATE
OF COMPLETION

THIS CERTIFICATE IS PROUDLY PRESENTED TO:

HAS SUCCESFULLY COMPLETED

The Siren Head Coloring Book

DATE

DUAA PRESS PUBLISHING

Made in the USA
Las Vegas, NV
13 September 2024

95240609R00044